Discover Sedona

A Local's Guide on
What to Do and Why

By Julian Martin Ross

Copyright 2018

Table of Contents

Preface

My first college roommate and I, together sporting the disposable income of your average toddler, signed up for cable television. We assumed we'd have it for at least two months before it would be cut off for nonpayment, but that was enough time to execute our plan. Some of the channels were running movie marathons, and we each had a healthy stash of VHS tapes we'd be okay with recording over. Our clever scheme would net us a healthy stash of movies and whatnot we could watch whenever we were supposed to be studying for the five or six years we assumed it'd take us to graduate.

Our first, and arguably best, haul on this scheme was all the original "Planet of the Apes" movies. Classics all. We recorded a good 40 hours of tv while that particular iron was hot, but one thing I'd recorded in particular wound up on repeat over my years at school. The Discovery Channel had aired a documentary about "Weird Sedona", and I'd forgotten to stop the recording after the "Aliens built the pyramids" thing before it.

From the very first clip I was thoroughly captivated - I'd never heard of Sedona before this show, and had no clue there was a place on our planet that looked anything close to that. Shot after shot of these otherworldly mountains and canyons, just the stuff of dreams, borderline psychedelic. It was the pinnacle of beautiful to me and a clinical obsession with the place warmly took over my being.

I briefly dated a girl solely because she'd transferred from Northern Arizona University and could entertain me with stories about Sedona. It was a sickness.

After school ended I took a job and made some money. I talked my college roommate, who moonlighted as my best friend, and a coworker on a grand adventure - we'd go to Sedona to celebrate New Year's Eve, 1999. If Y2K were going to hit, I'd rather fight off cannibals in those red rocks than in the Midwest. So at the end of December we piled into my buddy's car and drove the thousand plus miles to Red Rock Country.

No matter what direction you drive into town, there's one turn in particular on each highway that makes you quit talking, makes you turn down the radio and roll down the windows and go "Look..." thoroughly incorrect in any assumption that the others in the car aren't just as lost in awe as you are. And it only gets about a million times better from there.

The views from uptown and the airport. The food, the architecture, even the way the air felt. The desert hippie girls, the helicopter rides, the quiet contemplation alongside Oak Creek. Every single moment couldn't be topped, until it was by the next one.

We went to a New Year's Eve party at a local venue, filled ourselves with alcohol and rang in the new year sitting around roaring fire pits. And when we all shouted "Happy New Year!" at the top of our lungs, the first snowflakes of the year's first snow began to appear. I'm not prone to hyperbole but this was a magical moment.

We woke up to snowy peaks and postcard scenes, packed our bags and headed home. The following Friday I made the 2000 mile round trip to see it again. And also one of those desert hippie girls. But mostly it was for the scenery.

I came back a couple times a year for the following four years until fate intervened. My company lost a major client and half the staff would be laid off, including me. My last day was on a Wednesday, and on that Friday I was living in Sedona.

My visits over the years in no way prepared me for what I'd experience living here, which has been a string of bizarre, unsettling, unforgettable, amazing moments. They'd take up another book, a large one, and at some point I'll write them down like I've been saying I'd do for the past ten years. So in lieu of that, I wanted to focus on ways any given visitor can create their own moments here by sharing everything I think could be useful for anyone unfamiliar with the area.

This doesn't have a thorough breakdown of all the hiking and biking trails. There are free maps for that. This is more high level, things I wish someone had told me on that first trip, with some insight that's come from living around these wonderful weirdos for a stretch. I'll bet there's going to be more than enough in here to help you ensure that any visit to the area will stick with you for a very long time in a very powerful way.

When is the best time to visit?

Typical of the high desert, Sedona sees major temperature swings throughout the year. We're at 4300 ft. elevation, 3/5 of a mile higher than Phoenix and 2/3rds that of Flagstaff. We don't see the former's brutal summers or the latter's considerable snowfall, but we do experience swings of about 70 degrees throughout the year. Where winters see averages of highs in the 50s and lows in the 30s, summers bring highs toying with 100 and lows in the 60s. Summer days can be extreme but unlike humid places, the temperatures reliably cool off after sunset even on the hottest days.

But you want to be here when it's beautiful all day long, and that's when our tourist season occurs. Our most popular months for visitors are April and October, and we can always count on March through May and September through November being very, very busy times for the town.

April and October both see highs in the 70s and lows in the 40s, perfect for day hikes and scenic exploration during the days and relaxing by the fire (pretty much everywhere you go will likely have one going) in the evenings. Autumn is particularly popular here because the fall colors in the canyon are something out of a movie, just indescribably stellar.

If you do come during peak times, do know that you'll be here with the hundreds of thousands who thought similarly, so be prepared. Traffic in this town can turn into an ugly nightmare when everyone descends upon Sedona. Parking is often nonexistent and shuttles will be required.

Every parking spot at every trail head will be filled from the moment the sun appears to the moment it sets. Finding a table at a restaurant can require surprisingly long waits at times, and once seated, servers can't give their full attention in any given direction. Anticipate craziness and be surprised if you hit a brief lull - don't expect the town to make room for you.

A very popular, ridiculously scenic hiking spot is West Fork, a few miles up in Oak Creek Canyon. Cars start lining up in the canyon to be the first in, and this can lead to major delays in heading up the canyon. West Fork is one of the hardest places for anyone to visit during high season, so if you are hellbent on checking it out, make plans to visit during the off season - or plan on driving up the canyon well before it opens to claim your place in line.

Oak Creek Canyon itself has been rated as one of the top ten drives in the nation, and it's worth the trip up to the rim and back down if you haven't seen it before. It's only about 20 miles long, and there's a wonderful observation area at the top.

My personal preference is the view coming down, as the viewing distance afforded through the switchbacks is stunning, and when you hit the transition between canyon walls and red rock formations, it's like you're driving into a painting. But you can't go wrong either way.

 *One word of caution - it seems that every year we hear of someone from out of state going off the road and into very steep, dangerous canyons. Rescue teams appear in the local paper far too often, so make sure you stay off the front page of the Red Rock News. The speed limits posted in the canyon aren't highway "suggestions", they're absolutely crucial to staying on the road.

Hardly anyone ever encounters the complete 180s in the switchbacks and don't slow down half as much as they need to when approaching. Don't assume you know what you're getting into when heading up or down Oak Creek Canyon - pay careful attention to the posted speed limits and stay at or under them. I promise you, it'll make the rest of your time out here much more enjoyable.

Winters in Sedona are often very mild, and we'll only see snow cover the rock formations (which is jaw droppingly beautiful). The roads in town rarely get bad enough to affect driving, but it can happen. When snow is in the area, heading north from town is an entirely different story.

If you visit during the winter, ALWAYS check the forecast in Flagstaff before heading north, because the snow up there can turn into a total Michael Bay movie. You don't even want to think about trying the canyon when there is ice and snow on the road, and I-17 sees tractor trailer accidents yearly because of heavy accumulation.

It's hard to overstate how significant the snow can get in Flagstaff. Unless you're very experienced driving in such conditions and have a vehicle capable of handling it, don't begin to think it's a good idea to roll the dice on a trip through heavy snow in and around Flag.

Monsoon Season

Our monsoon season runs from June through September. This can bring pleasant afternoon showers to cut through the heat, cloud cover that's perfect for a hike, or it can bring torrential rainfall that floods every creek, cuts off road access and threatens lives. I've personally seen a flash flood here reduce a home to its foundation, pick up an RV and carry it downstream, and knock out bridges. This season also brings with it a significant number of lighting strikes, which can lead to wildfires or worse. Make sure you check the weather before making plans to be outside this time of year.

But I have to tell you - the sunsets. Oh, the sunsets. In all my travels across the country, never in my life have I consistently seen sunsets like what we can get here. I've seen restaurants empty of patrons so they can all go see the unreal colors and huge rainbows arching over the rocks. If you are a camera aficionado, this is an outstanding time to be around town.

The water is up everywhere, which makes for awesome shots along Oak Creek, the pools fill atop the Secret Trail slick rock (one of the most famous spots to photograph Cathedral Rock) and the clouds are like paintings. Everyone looks forward to monsoon season for a variety of reasons, but my favorite by far is the heavenly skies they bring with them.

Full Moon and New Moon

Both of these have their advantages and disadvantages around Sedona. The full moon is spectacular when it arcs over town, and the illumination can make for unforgettable night hiking opportunities. As well, the locals have a huge drum circle at Cathedral Rock every full moon when the weather is tolerable, and if you have some hippie in you, you'll get the full Sedona experience by wandering up the trail to the Cathedral Rock plateau off Back O' Beyond Road and listening in.

The new moon brings with it a particularly wonderful experience - the stars as you'd see them in the middle of nowhere, billions of them, a sky so completely packed with stars that it's hard to comprehend, especially if you are used to the light poisoning of a major city. Sedona has been designated as a member of the International Dark Sky Community, a group of cities that enact legislation designed to eliminate light pollution at night. And it sure shows.

When the moon is bright it can diminish the number of stars you can see, but during a new moon or a sliver of a crescent moon, you'll need to make time to head somewhere you can experience this. You could even just step outside a hotel room to see the Milky Way stretching above you. If you enjoy astrophotography, plan to be here during a new moon.

The downside to the Dark Sky Community approach, during the new moon, is that it gets DARK outside. It's not just smart to have some sort of flashlight with you, it can mean the difference between finding your car and stumbling into a cactus. That's no exaggeration. Most cell phones nowadays come with, or can download free versions of, flashlight apps so make sure you have one ready to go if you're here during this time.

Getting to Sedona by Car

Since pretty much everyone arrives in Sedona via something with wheels on it, I'm going to start out by rating the ways you can get into town.

From Cottonwood

The drive from Cottonwood along 89A provides a massive panoramic view of the Verde Valley and the red rocks nestled within. Bonus points if you start up in Jerome because the views up there will knock the breath out of you. The big reveal, when you reach Red Rock Loop Rd., is awesome, especially because you are instantly in town. There's no bad way to see Sedona, but this is my least favorite means to do so.

Rating: 7.1

From Highway 179

If you're driving up from Phoenix, your first opportunity to get to Sedona is exiting I-17 at Highway 179. This is a nice road to take in, as it has a great buildup to it. It'll take you twelve or so minutes to reach the outskirts of the Village of Oak Creek, essentially a Sedona suburb, and you'll get your first red rock views in the form of Bell Rock and Courthouse Butte in the near distance. The little town itself is a neat little spot where you can get gas, food, etc. and head through the remaining four miles to Sedona.

Once you head out of town the scenery will start to assault you, and your first view of Cathedral Rock from the east will push you over the edge a bit. It's a great drive into town (although if you come at the height of tourist season, you may get to enjoy this drive at approximately four miles an hour thanks to crazy traffic).

Rating 8.8

Through Oak Creek Canyon

If you're coming from the north, or if you really want to delay your arrival if coming from the south, you can take 89A from I-17 just south of Flagstaff. The first seven or eight miles is straightforward, through the massive pine forest, and there's a great lookout point right when you get to the edge of the canyon's rim. From there it quickly descends (literally and figuratively) into a death-tempting series of switchbacks right out of a video game. They're super fun to drive. You'll snake through the canyon, ranked by USA Today some years ago as one of the 10 most beautiful drives in America, for a number of miles. And then, when you get near enough, the red rocks start relentlessly overpowering your senses, and then you'll see the Sedona welcome sign, and then you'll see Uptown and the wall of magical mountains, and then you'll start laughing because you just can't process your emotions by this point. Highly recommended.

Rating 9.7

Down Schnebly Hill

Saving the best for last here. Back a hundred years or so, the way into this new little haven was via Schnebly Hill Road. It's always been a dirt road, and over the decades it's become a brutally rocky path down. I can't emphasize this enough - this road sucks BAD. Four wheel drives are recommended for it, but I've made it in high-clearance two wheel drives.

You'll need to take it at about five miles an hour so you can dodge the thousand unnecessarily large rocks waiting to consume your oil pan, and it's stressful, and it's probably safest to not even think about taking it unless you have a lifted suspension or serious experience driving offroad. But holy Hell, absent almost all hyperbole, is it the best thing ever. There are turns along this road that will make you want to puke up all that road trip beef jerky, will slow you down miserably if anyone in your party has a camera available.

The total lack of guard rails, coupled with steep cliffs falling hundreds of feet, will make anyone on the passenger side want to rig up some kind of diaper. And it's so damn beautiful that it's worth every sweat-inducing second of the arduous drive down. This is hands down the best possible way to get into Sedona. I would live up here if I could.

Rating: Forty solid gold Kachina dolls with sparkling diamond eyes wrapped in hundred dollar bills

Red Rock Pass

Many years ago, to address a serious need for scenic restoration funding (trail maintenance, park staffing, anything scenic tourism-related), the city started requiring a Red Rock Pass to be purchased before visiting many popular places around town. Many locals lost their collective mind. They were completely dumbfounded that they'd have to pay to walk the trails they'd been on for years, sometimes decades, and went so far as to hire an attorney to discover loopholes in the wording they could use to their advantage (he did, and they do).

This won't apply to you, so just know that if you want to park any pretty much any trail head around town you're going to need one of these things. They're currently $5 a day, $15 for a week or $20 for a year. You can also get a grand pass for $40 that also includes access to Grasshopper Point, Crescent Moon Ranch and Call Of The Canyon Picnic Area. There are a handful of locations that don't accept the pass, such as West Fork, so be prepared to pay entrance fees to access some of the amenities.

You can pick up a pass at the Chamber of Commerce Visitors' Center located uptown, at most convenience stores, and many trail heads and parking areas have self-serve kiosks. Depending on how you buy yours, you'll either get a hang tag for your rear view mirror or a printed ticket that you'll leave on your dash when leaving your car unattended.

Do note that the city doesn't require a pass for what they consider incidental parking, such as stopping at a vista or to take a couple of photos. But if you're going to be away from your vehicle for any substantial amount of time, make sure a pass is displayed in a readable way. The rangers check for them, and they do issue fines for vehicles without one. It's a very cheap way to avoid any problems and help support those who maintain these areas for maximum enjoyment.

The Areas of Sedona

This is a quick overview of the various areas that comprise Sedona, to help you navigate and put together a game plan for a solid time in the area. Many tourist locations will be briefly touched upon here to place them in context with the town as a whole and will be expounded upon in later sections.

Uptown

This is the first part of town you'll encounter if coming down through Oak Creek Canyon, and is just north of the roundabout where 89A and 179 connect, right next to the Hyatt Residence Club and Pinon Pointe shopping area. Uptown is tourist ground zero, completely overloaded with souvenir shops, t-shirt stores, galleries, cafes & restaurants and whatever else someone can dream up to take your money. It's well worth at least one visit, just to experience it, even if you don't go in any of the shops.

The views are awesome here, the area is fun to explore, and there are many genuinely interesting places to check out. You'll find places to sign up for offroad and air tours here, and if you have the time and budget, do both, with a Jeep ride at a minimum. Just be aware that everyone in the area is there to sell you something, whether it initially feels like it or not, so just go into any encounter expecting it to take a turn toward some sales pitch. Want a timeshare? You'll have twelve offers if you are friendly enough to people standing in front of their shops.

If you arrive in uptown during tourist season, you'll likely find every single parking spot along the main drag to be taken. Recently the town made these metered parking, so be prepared to pay if you're lucky enough to snag one. Fortunately, there's an abundance of public parking on either side of 89A, some free all day and some free for 3 hours. Keep an eye out for the public parking direction signs along the way and you'll find something available.

When things look busy, I don't want to hop from lot to lot looking for spots, so my go-to one is off Schnebly Rd. It's the largest one available, and a two minute walk to the shops, and I've always found a spot there. You can get to this one by taking Jordan Rd at the south end of uptown and taking a right on Schnebly Rd. The entrance will be on your left. This lot is one of the "free all day" lots so you don't have to worry about time limitations if you get caught up exploring.

The visitors' center is located on the south end of uptown, on the south side of Forest Rd. It's worth stopping in if you aren't familiar with the area - you can get maps and brochures here, and the center is always staffed with people very knowledgeable about the area.

Just south of the visitors' center is Pinon Pointe, which is a little more upscale. There's a Starbucks here, if that's an essential thing to you. The views are really nice here with the extra elevation and it's usually not nearly as crowded as uptown proper.

Tlaquepaque (pronounced Tuh-lack-uh-packy)

In my opinion, a must-visit area in town, especially if you haven't seen it before. If you have seen it before, but it's been a while, know that Tlaquepaque North has been built across 179 and features new galleries and a restaurant. The developer of this project sent a team of architects throughout Mexico to document every detail of Mexican artist villages, which they very faithfully recreated here.

The authentic Spanish Colonial design, with its intricate ironwork, cobblestone streets and stunning courtyards really feel like another country. This is one of my favorite places to wander about when things calm down in the evenings, with Oak Creek meandering nearby and red rocks visible over the trees. While I don't subscribe to any of the New Age aspects of the town, I must say that there's some kind of vibe that seems to emanate from this area that keeps pulling me back in to enjoy it even more.

The food in Tlaquepaque is consistently fantastic and the shops are oriented toward higher-end galleries and boutique shops. It just feels classy, a nice palate cleanser after experiencing the retail assault of uptown. Also, a few times a year Tlaquepaque holds most excellent festivals, such as Dia de los Muertes, and for a good portion of the year hosts the farmers' market. Check their website for a schedule of events - if there's something awesome going on there, the parking disappears in about 47 seconds, but whatever it is will be worth having to park elsewhere and take a tram in or walk. They go all out for their events, bringing in absolutely wonderful musicians, dancers and performers, and there's never been an event there that I didn't thoroughly enjoy.

Fun fact: the concept of Tlaquepaque was that of an artists' village, where the artist would live upstairs and show their work on the lower level. When the complex opened in the 70s, they put this into play, allowing for visitors to see the artists at work and talk with them. Locals soon discovered, however, that when you provide a bunch of artists a place to live together, they tend to live it up in spectacular ways once the sun set, and due to the incessant parties and subsequent noise, they were all politely asked to get the hell out so they could convert their living quarters to additional gallery spaces. You win some, you lose some. At least it wound up leading to more interesting places to visit.

West Sedona

From a tourist's standpoint, West Sedona encompasses the area around Airport Rd. to Red Rock Loop Rd. on 89A. This is the meat of Sedona, where most people live, but has a fair amount of draw for visitors as well.

Airport Road leads to two must-visit locations - the AIrport Saddle and Airport Vista. Climbing the hill at the saddle is the easiest way to get some of the best views of Sedona as a whole, and driving to the top allows visitors to see the famous stretch of red rocks to the west of West Sedona, including the iconic Thunder Mountain. After Airport Road you'll find Soldiers Pass Rd, which takes you past and through some stunning neighborhoods to the Soldiers Pass trail head.

Next up, Posse Grounds Rd will take you to one of the dog parks, a bike skills park for adventurous mountain bikers and a surprisingly nice skate park. West of Posse Grounds, tourists will find many excellent restaurants, grocery stores, gas stations, our movie theatre and many businesses that cater to locals. If you're vegan, I highly recommend checkout ChocolaTree, especially if it's nice enough to sit in their outdoor area.

At the intersection of Coffee Pot Dr. and 89A you'll find Coffee Pot Restaurant. This is one of our more famous locations, going strong since the 1950s and is highly recommended as a breakfast spot. Their claim to fame is a menu featuring 101 omelettes, of which I've eaten well over half the list and have never had anything less than an awesome breakfast experience. I like sitting on the smoke-free patio when the weather allows.

However, its popularity is equal to its fame, and scoring a table may require throwing a few punches or being extremely patient. During normal breakfast hours you will not find a parking spot available, so the only way I've found I can reliably get a table there when it's busy is to go pretty early or for brunch. They're open 6am-2pm, and if you try to go between 8 and 11 you're going to get grumpy due to the crowd.

If you're more spiritually inclined, or just want to take in all the Sedona flavor you can, it's worth a visit to the Amitabha Stupa and Peace Park near the end of Andante Drive (approximately a half mile up, then turn left on Pueblo Drive to see the entrance). Considered to be representative of the Buddha when he achieved enlightenment, the 36 ft. Amitabha and smaller Tara Stupas are popular spots for prayer and contemplation. Regardless as to your personal beliefs, it's a beautiful little park that's undeniably peaceful and makes for a great photo op.

Another quarter mile to the west and you'll find Dry Creek Rd. This will take you back into the Secret Mountain Wilderness Area with access to many trail heads, including the famous Boynton Canyon Trail near Enchantment Resort. After Dry Creek, the next road that brings rewards for visitors is Upper Red Rock Loop Road. This road loops around and reconnects with 89A after a 15 minute drive, allowing you to easily get back into town, and it is one of my favorite drives in Sedona. I personally think you need to start on the upper side, near the high school, to fully appreciate the views.

Not long after the high school you'll find a vista with unimproved parking. This affords a wonderful sweeping view of Cathedral Rock and the surrounding scenery and should not be missed. If you only have time to make it down to this one vista, make sure it's on your list of things to see. As you progress around the loop you'll have access to Secret Slickrock Trail, Crescent Moon State Park and Red Rock State Park. Beyond that you'll have a beautiful, easy drive back to 89A and into town.

West of Red Rock Loop Rd., you'll have a 10 mile stretch of highway that will take you to Page Springs and its excellent wineries, Cornville, which has a handful of restaurants far better than what you'd expect at first glance, and then another six miles to Cottonwood. Beyond there, it's another four miles to Jerome.

Highway 179

Just beyond Tlaquepaque you'll run into another roundabout. From here you can continue south on 179, or you can head north up Schnebly Hill Road. If you've read the section on ways to get into Sedona, you will have an appreciation for what a brutal driving experience much of Schnebly Hill is, but from the roundabout you'll have a paved road for about a mile.

If you just want to take in the views, it's worth driving up to the trail head parking lot to get a great view of uptown and the scenery from the northeast. If you are up for hiking, you have access to a number of excellent trails starting here. But it's as far as you'll be able to go without four wheel drive.

Staying on 179 past the roundabout will take you by a handful of galleries, including Exposures, the largest in the state. You'll know it before you see the sign - the artwork out front is always so impressive that it'll make it hard to focus on the road. Many famous artists choose Exposures as home for their work, and you'll never have a bad time visiting there. You should check their calendar of events, as they have a variety of interesting things hosted there. One visit I was able to observe a group of Buddhist monks visiting from Asia constructing a beautifully intricate sand mandala.

Just beyond Exposures is Hillside. This area has my personal favorite Mexican restaurant, Javelina Cantina, partially because I love sitting on their patio. The views are even better from the restaurant at the top level, currently The Hudson. As for the shops, it's hit or miss. This area used to be full of great shops but has been in decline for a while - my last visit there found many spaces unoccupied. It's worth visiting just to go to either restaurant and check out the views from the upper levels, but it's not a must-see area to visit.

Roughly a mile south of Hillside you'll find Chapel Rd. which will take you to the Chapel of the Holy Cross, one of the most visited spots in town. This famous icon has been perched among the red rocks since the 1950s, and I consider it a must-see location. The chapel itself is fascinating and unique, and the location chosen to build it is as beautiful as anywhere you'll visit in town.

The next roundabout south of Chapel Rd will take you to Back O' Beyond Rd. Many famous actors and musicians are rumored to live in this area, and it leads to the Cathedral Rock trail, one of my favorite places to go hiking and walking. You get an excellent view of Cathedral Rock from the highway, but it's almost criminal to enjoy it solely by driving by. I recommend checking it out on foot from one of the famous vantage points, of which this is one. The others I'll cover specifically under the Cathedral Rock section.

South of Back O' Beyond, you'll continue for about a mile before you reach the parking area for Bell Rock and Courthouse Butte. I personally love getting high up on Bell Rock to enjoy the views, but I'll caution that it requires confidence and coordination in footing. It's not an area for the faint of heart. I also definitely do not recommend biting off more than you can chew if you attempt to explore Bell Rock - I've witnessed a number of helicopter rescues off the formation, as tourist after tourist thinks they can get up - and back down - from precarious spots.

At the very top of Bell Rock, there is apparently a metal box with a notebook and pencil in it for climbers to record their ascent, and I know many who have signed that book. But making it to the very top is definite "gamble with death" territory and do NOT recommend considering it unless you're a very experienced climber.

The Village of Oak Creek

South of Bell Rock another quarter mile, you'll find the northern boundary of the Village of Oak Creek. It's a sleepy little offshoot of Sedona, where many locals live, and while there are some great hotels and wonderful restaurants in the area, it's not crucial that you budget time to explore the amenities. It does feature The Collective Sedona at the southern end, a nice collection of galleries and restaurants, worth checking out if you're in the mood, but not a must-see destination spot. The one thing that consistently pulls me over to VOC (what we call it) is access to Oak Creek Crossing and the wonderful view of Cathedral Rock. It's easily one of the top iconic spots in town and I'll be frustrated if I learn you didn't make time to visit it in some fashion. I'll get into that more in the Cathedral Rock section, but just know that if you're planning on being in VOC, this is a great start for a visit to Oak Creek's most famous spot.

There are many really great restaurants in the area - Cucina Rustica is a fantastic Italian place and Minami can't be beat for sushi, and the upswing is that most tourists stay close to their Sedona hotels, so it can be easier to get a table out in VOC. When I would regularly visit the area before I moved here, I would occasionally choose to stay in VOC, as I could find better hotel rates, and the drive into Sedona is so wonderful and quick that I didn't feel as though I were diminishing the experience in any way at all.

South of The Collective is the southern boundary of VOC and nothing but highway to reach I-17. If you're in this area and would like to explore Cornville, Page Springs, Cottonwood or Jerome, you can head south a couple of miles to Beaverhead Flat Rd., which will take you over six miles of high desert to Cornville Rd. From there, it's a quick jaunt to the north to enter Cornville and Page Springs, and if you stay on Cornville Rd. it will lead you right to the outskirts of Cottonwood, intersecting with 89A.

A Little Further Out

Cornville

Cornville is a tiny community about fifteen miles from Sedona, and is not a tourist destination. If you find yourself driving through the town, you likely won't stop unless it's at a gas station. If you do find yourself in the area and are hungry, there are some absolutely great restaurants, my personal favorites being Vince's, Manzanita, and Grasshopper Grill. Watch that speedometer like a hawk when driving through here - speed limits drop fast, down to 25, and there's probably a radar gun on you even if the place looks completely deserted.

Page Springs

Page Springs is the hub of the northern Arizona winery explosion as of late, and award-winning wines are pouring (pun intended) out of the area. With most residing off of Oak Creek, you're going to find surprisingly great wine, food and scenery all in one place. If you want to put some time into the offerings in the area, look up info on the Verde Valley Wine Trail. I could write another guide just on wine in the area, so I'll let all the considerable info on this area already out there serve as additional education and guidance.

One restaurant in particular you should check out in the area is Up The Creek restaurant, right in the middle of Page Springs. Well worth the drive.

Cottonwood

Cottonwood is the low key, laid back slightly bigger brother to Sedona. It's where many people live who work in, but can't afford to live in, Sedona proper. It has an Old Town district, where the old downtown area has undergone a complete makeover, with excellent restaurants, galleries and gift shops. Old Town is great if you're looking for something to check out but it isn't an essential part of a visit to the Verde Valley.

If you do want to explore Old Town, I recommend Crema for breakfast and coffee, Nic's for a classier (and delicious) dining experience, and the Tavern Grille. Arizona Stronghold Vineyards and Merkin Vineyards both have great wine and food.

If you like kayaking and canoeing, the Verde River runs right through town. Much bigger than Oak Creek, it's a really solid paddling experience with great high desert views. Bring your own boats or rent from local providers here and in Clarkdale. Use your fancy internet to learn more.

Cottonwood has a Super Walmart, which was the main reason I'd visit when I was a tourist. Sedona's pretty self sufficient but there are certain things you just need to track down a Walmart for. Most of the time Cottonwood is a waypoint on the way up to Jerome, which lives for tourism.

Clarkdale

From Cottonwood, you can either continue on Main St. through Old Town or up 89A on your way to Jerome to find the very small community of Clarkdale. If you're after a particularly unique way of experiencing the local scenery, the depot for the Verde Canyon Railroad is here, which is a very fun - but pricey - way to take in the scenery. If you're looking for a great way to kill about 4 hours, this is an excellent option.

Aside from the train, there's no other compelling reason to visit. Interesting to drive through if you're meandering around the area, but it's just not a draw like other areas. However, if you've totally fallen in love with the area and are determined to move out here, like thousands before you, it's a great, quiet area to live in - if you don't mind driving into Cottonwood for basically every single thing.

Jerome

I'm deeply in love with the tiny community of Jerome, so my review is deservedly under "Nearby Places to Visit" rather than here. It's less of a town than a thing to experience, which I think anyone who comes out for a visit should do.

Tourist Essentials

While some trips to the area revolve around more focused agendas, I wanted to offer what I consider to be the best way to get an all-around general experience of what Sedona has to offer.

*To revisit a note in the preface, in case you skipped it: I'm not getting into detail on hiking and biking trails in this guide. Each of those would require a separate book due to the volume of options and info available. If you are planning to do either of those heavily, there are so many outstanding resources on each that I'd just be regurgitating that info. Do some online research on trail difficulty for each, and if you're here with your mountain bike, visit one of the local shops to get personalized recommendations.

Bare Essential

Walk around Uptown for an hour minimum. It's generally hectic, parking is often a mess, and it's just a blatant tourist trap, but when I'm up there I have to hang up my cynicism and just enjoy the hell out of it. The views from uptown are stellar, there are a bunch of interesting shops to check out, and the vibe is consistently really positive. Solid food options (especially the Cowboy Club and Thai Palace, my two go-to spots uptown), good coffee, a lot of courtyard sitting to take in the scene. You're invariably surrounded by people who are excited to be there, so the mood is high, people are friendly, and it's an iconic spot for the town. It's worth going just to walk the sidewalks for a bit and see everything, even if you have no intention of shopping or eating.

Cruise through Tlaquepaque at any time it's open. It's too interesting to miss. It's not that big, you could walk the whole grounds in twenty minutes if you didn't go in any shops, but you'd be missing out if you went that route. Absolutely amazing art is on display throughout this area, and the food is great to wonderful - Rene is tops, El Rincon is a popular Mexican spot and the Oak Creek Brewery makes fantastic beer (have to mention their amber, it's one of my favorites anywhere when it's from the tap). The area is just overflowing with "good energy", take that how you will, and needs to be seen. I just find it beautiful and inspiring and will stop in to meander when I'm nearby. I love Tlaquepaque.

Visit the Airport Overlook. The view from this vantage point is one of the most iconic in the area, and the overlook is only 50 feet or so from the paid parking area ($3 last visit). Break out your camera and be ready to wait your turn for an unobstructed view, but for quick visits this gets you the essential Sedona scenic experience.

Drive to the Village of Oak Creek on Highway 179. Just drive down, swing around the first roundabout and head back in. This will take you 20 minutes if traffic isn't being stupid, and it's nonstop jaw-dropping scenery.

Drive to Red Rock Loop Rd. at the west end of West Sedona and take it a few hundred feet down to a spectacular overlook. After you pass the high school the road will curve to the right - keep going past the first dirt parking area. You'll make a quick turn to the left, and you'll see a bigger dirt parking area on the left, with a smaller one on the right. This is where you want to stop. This is a fast and cheap way to see Cathedral Rock and the area formations. You might run into me here - I'll take a lawn chair out here when it's nice, just to enjoy the view while I do some writing.

That's my bare minimum recommendation. If you have more time available, the following list will help you make that much more of your trip out here.

Essentially Essential

When I say bare essentials, I truly mean "we had just enough time to do X, Y, Z and next time we're absolutely going to have to do A, B, C." Anything less than the above is little more than looking at a postcard. But most people in the area have more time available that what the above will take, so this is my "actual essentials" list. This list is in addition to, or in one case replacing, what's above.

Make the short climb to Sedona Airport Vortex. While it would be agonizing to have to choose my absolute favorite view in town, I know without a doubt this area ties for first place. The 360 degree views are very easy to reach, and the scenery you can take in will cover a major swath of the red rocks. Head up Airport Road, and right when the road heads to the left you'll find a parking area that requires a Red Rock Pass (and has a kiosk to buy one).

There's no set trail to get to the top of the hill there referred to as the Vortex, just make your way up however seems safest. While it's stunning during the day, this is my go-to place when it's dark and the stars are out. Coming from a city with massive light pollution, I am consistently amazed with the combination of scenic silhouettes and positively magical number of stars you can see here.

While I don't subscribe to any of the local New Age practices and trends, I will say that this is my spot when I need to remember why I love it here so much. Spending a half hour up on this rock is the best thing I can do for peace and mental health. It's just wonderful beyond description and one of my favorite little spots on this planet.

The climb to the top of the hill isn't bad, but it isn't a walk in the park, either, even though it only takes a minute to climb up. While almost no one will have problems making it to the top, think twice about trying it if you're unsure on your feet or have balance issues. At the very least, be slow and deliberate with your footing.

This option can replace the visit to the Airport Overlook above. While it's only another minute up to this excellent vista, the views are essentially the same, although the Overlook gives a better view of West Sedona as a whole, especially at sunset when the town lights up. Doing both is ideal, as they're so close to one another, especially if you're collecting photos. But if you need to choose between the two, the Vortex trumps the Overlook as far as experiences go.

See Cathedral Rock in a more scenic setting. Getting a glimpse from the road just doesn't begin to do it justice. There are three ways to check it out, any one of which will treat you very well. Visiting all of them is ideal, but not necessary, and each provides such a nice view that I can't pick a favorite. I will say that #2 takes you to the one spot that provides what's considered the most iconic scenic shot in town, if you're after that experience or photo opportunity.

1. From Highway 179, between Sedona and VOC, take Back O' Beyond Rd. to the parking area/trail head. Remember to display your Red Rock Pass. This will

get you closest to Cathedral, with a trail that'll take you up as far as you want to go. The initial stretch is pretty flat, most people can make it, but it gets a lot trickier once you are up a ways. I like heading to the large slickrock area before the trail gets unnecessarily vertical - it has wonderful views of the red rocks and you'll get a pretty intimate view of Cathedral, seeing as you're a quarter up its side by that point. Templeton Trail is a level trail that runs flat alongside the formation, and it's worth walking a stretch of it even if you don't want to go all the way around.

2. From Red Rock Loop Road at the west end of West Sedona, take a left on Chavez Ranch Rd. and a right on Red Rock Crossing Rd. down to the Crescent Moon Picnic Area. There's a separate fee to get in here beyond the Red Rock Pass (unless you picked up the $40 deluxe pass) and it's worth five times the entrance fee.

   You'll see two looping parking areas - go to the one at the end of the road. You'll immediately have an excellent view of Cathedral Rock here, the famous shot with the wooden barn in the foreground, but for the full experience you'll need to take one of the two paths toward the treeline. When you reach the trees, there will be a couple easy ways to get over to the bank of Oak Creek. From this point, the Red Rock Crossing area, you'll be able to see Cathedral with Oak Creek curving in front of it, the iconic image you'll see accompanying essentially every story on the town. If you have some time to meander, there's a trail that follows the creek you can check out.

A word of warning, though - don't try to cross the creek if the water is up in any way, even the short distance to the slickrock island only 30-40 feet away. In this area, the bottom of the creek consists of large boulders in many places, and it's extremely easy to step in the water and immediately get dunked thanks to the slick inclines. I learned my lesson the hard way so you don't have to. If it's warm and you absolutely must give it a try, hand someone your wallet, purse, and phone before rolling those dice.

3. Last is my personal favorite, because of the large area you can explore. Head to VOC, down to the third roundabout and take Verde Valley School Rd. to the west (past the Chase Bank on the corner). You'll cut through a neighborhood on a paved road for about a mile, then onto a dirt road (but well maintained, no issues for passenger vehicles) for another 2/3 mile to a parking area on the left (again, Red Rock Pass time).

Park and continue down the road for 3-400 feet to Red Rock Crossing on the opposite side of Oak Creek from Crescent Moon. If it's heavy tourist season you may find this area to be a popular spot for swimmers and tourists in general. It's a wonderful place to get up close and personal with Oak Creek, and you can head north on Red Rock Crossing Trail to get some fantastic views. This trail connects with Baldwin trail, which is an easy loop through the immediate area, as well as Templeton Trail from my first option above if you want to explore further.

If you are diligently following this guide, you'll be venturing down the start of Red Rock Loop Rd. at some point, and I recommend you drive the whole thing. It doesn't take more than 20 minutes, and you'll wind up at 89A where you can take a right to head back into Sedona, or a left to head to Cottonwood/Jerome/Page Springs. When I drive to or from Cottonwood and have the extra time, I take this road just to appreciate where I'm living.

Take Schnebly Hill Rd. from the roundabout between Hillside Sedona and Tlaquepaque on Highway 179. About a mile up you'll run out of paved road at the parking area labeled "Huckaby and Margs Draw Trails". Red Rock pass required and a kiosk is available. If you're up for some trails, these are some personal favorites, but for this section, it's worth just walking back to the west and north of the lot and wandering around to enjoy the views. There's a good chance that by seeing all the amazing areas that Schnebly Hill Rd. leads into, it'll make you seriously consider one of the Jeep tours that will take you to the top.

Visit the Chapel of the Holy Cross. You can get there by heading on Highway 179 toward VOC. About a mile down you'll find the Chapel Rd. roundabout where you'll want to head east, toward the large rock formation. You'll see the Chapel not long after heading down Chapel Rd. Depending on how busy it is, you'll have parking options at the top of the road near the entrance or right after you cross the cattle guard. The views from this vantage point alone are worth the drive, and the chapel itself is a fascinating little structure to explore. It's such an iconic element of the Sedona experience that I highly recommend even a quick visit if you're in the area.

Round The Trip Out Perfectly

Take a Jeep tour. It's well worth it. Pink Jeep Tours is the most popular one in town, but any of them will do. Most of the most interesting places around town require a specialized vehicle to get there, and the drivers are extremely educated on what you'll be seeing. If you're interested in the history of the ancient Sinagua tribe, you can take tours to visit the cliff dwellings in the area. If you want just ridiculously wonderful scenery, take any tour that will get you on, and to the top of, Schnebly Hill.

The view from the vista up there is another "tied for first" for me (and there are many scenes on the way up that are "Tied for ever so slightly behind first"). And if you want awesome views and an adrenaline rush, book a tour that'll take you up Broken Arrow Trail. It's nature's roller coaster, intense and pure fun.

Visit Jerome. It's hard not to put this in the essential category, but I accept the fact that you can have a wonderful time without making the drive out to see it. The town was one of the things that totally hooked me on the area, though, and I'm hopelessly in love with every square inch of it, so I'm going to try to temper my hype only moderately. Read my bit about it under "Nearby Places to Visit".

Take in some history of the area. While the Jeep tours will get you to the cliff dwelling sites, you can visit them on your own quite easily. Some are down dirt roads that are all passable with passenger vehicles. We have Palatki and Honanki just outside Sedona, Tuzigoot just outside Cottonwood, and Montezuma's Castle and Well in Camp Verde and Rimrock.

If you're a serious history nerd, Wupatki is north of Flagstaff, about 90 minutes from Sedona, and is one of the most impressive - it's worth the drive if you're interested in this kind of thing. I have reviews on each of these places under "Nearby Places to Visit".

Take a hike anywhere. There are numerous free trail guides available online, at the visitors' center and at various local shops. You don't have to be a hardcore hiker to enjoy a sampling of what I've been told is more than 80 miles of trails in the area. Find something that's your speed - you don't have to do the whole thing, just enough to get a perspective on the landscape that's only available on foot. Some easy ones to start out with are Boynton Canyon, Airport Loop Trail and Bell Rock Trail.

If it's warm out, brave the crowds at Slide Rock State Park. A very scenic spot where you can enjoy Oak Creek, this area has a really nice series of swimming holes carved out of the red rocks. You can slide down a chute polished so smooth by eons of erosion that, depending on how much water is coming down the canyon, you'll be pushed along by the force of the water.

It's a very beautiful spot, another area icon, but if you're looking for more of a solitary experience you won't find it here. It can get wildly popular when it's hot out, and you can run into hundreds out here. I personally have never seen it so crowded that it detracts from enjoying the spot, but that doesn't mean it isn't a possibility. Slide Rock State Park sits about 5 miles up Oak Creek Canyon from Uptown.

Upgrade to Deluxe

If you're here with kids, or if you like a mixture of exotic animals and a adrenaline, take a look at Out of Africa Wildlife Park outside Camp Verde, 10 miles south of Cottonwood. They offer bush safari trips to see free-roaming African wildlife, very similar to what you'd expect on a trip to Tanzania. You can feed a tiger, check out wildlife shows, and try your hand at my all-time personal favorite - a zipline course that runs over the sanctuary, allowing you to sail over the heads of giraffes, rhinos and other exotics.

It's a completely different feel from a zoo, and you'll appreciate the animals living somewhere more akin to their habitat. Worth the cost and drive out. If you're looking for a very rewarding way to kill a few hours, check out their website for all the details.

If you're in Sedona, the fastest way to get there is by taking Highway 179 through VOC to I-17, heading south for approximately ten miles, then turning right/northwest on Highway 260. You'll find it about 3 miles up on your left. If you're out in/near Cottonwood, take 89A to 260, which is Main St. in town, right by the Taco Bell and Giant Gas Station. Head south on 260 about ten miles and you'll find it on your right.

Get in the air. Since the air tours are a bit more of a luxury, they're the best possible way to take in the area. I love the helicopter flights and balloon trips, and while my particular set of nerves have kept me out of the cockpit of one of the available biplanes, I've heard too many breathlessly giddy and glowing reviews about the experience.

Bonus: If you're a photographer like me, some of the air tour companies offer "doors off" flights so you can get unimpeded shots that will make other shooters want to throw away their gear. Super worth it. And if you're up for seeing the Grand Canyon from a wonderfully unique perspective, you can fly out of Sedona Airport to experience the canyon from above.

Do you find architecture fascinating? Are you a Star Wars fan that has always wanted to wander the streets of a city out of the movie? If so, you need to carve out some time to visit Arcosanti. This "city of the future" lies about 45 minutes south of Sedona just off of I-17 at the intersection of Highway 69. My full write up of this fascinating area is under "Nearby Places to Visit".

Sedona's Traffic Roundabouts

I'm going to assume you've never driven in a roundabout, or traffic circle, as it appears that 94% of our visitors find them as alien as the flying visitors we apparently put up with. Between Sedona and the Village of Oak Creek we have eight for you to attempt, so knowing what you're getting into before you approach one will keep our traffic accident count to a reasonable level.

Approach the roundabout. If no other vehicles are present, drive on in. If vehicles are present in the circle, you have to yield to them, only moving once sufficient space is available. Pay attention where your lane goes - for some, the outer lane goes straight and the inner lane keeps turning. If you're in the inner lane and realize you need to go straight, do not whip into the outer lane. This is the maneuver that seems to cause more accidents and injuries than anything else.

Take a turn around the loop, signal a lane change and move over to get where you're going. Same goes for moving from the outer to the inner loop. At almost every roundabout you'll be able to get wherever you want to go by being in the outer loop, so get in the right lane before you get too near one if you're uncomfortable navigating them. And remember EVERY SINGLE ONE will turn to the right for everyone, so for the love of God don't get a wild hair and see how turning left works out for you. I can tell you confidently that it won't.

Our traffic accidents and injuries have plummeted thanks to the switch from street lights and intersections to roundabouts. But every tourist season brings a rash of terrible drivers who have the worst possible time trying to figure them out on the fly, which necessitates bringing this up. My apologies if this sounds condescending but if you live here for any length of time you'll just want to steal car keys from about every other person you're driving near in one of these. Be smart - be part of the solution, not part of the problem.

Nearby Places to Visit

Jerome

After the discovery of two massive copper deposits up the mountain in the late 1800's, Jerome developed from a small camp to a city of thousands, helping to turn the area into Arizona's highest-producing mine and one of the largest mines in the world. The mine saw ups and downs into the 30's, when the operation was crippled by plummeting copper prices, and the end of mining in the early 50's left Jerome as little more than a ghost town.

Curious visitors to the area helped to bring the town back to life, and over decades of work to revive the area, it's now home to around 450. Visitors get to experience a very unique town that still has many elements of its origin in mining. Buildings from the past century still stand, in various states of repair, all throughout the little town.

As it is built on a mountain slope, homes are situated with their foundations level with the rooftops of the ones below them, and there is no location in town that doesn't require some sort of climb. Today it's a combination of crumbling ghost town and ultra-quirky mountain village, with too much wonderfully weird vibe to process.

And the views! It's worth the drive up even if you don't get out of your car (which would be a terrible idea). You can see Flagstaff's Humphrey Peak from the town, with scenery stretching for 50 plus miles to the east. The views are so stellar here that I'll go up just to walk the old sidewalks and take in everything I can see. It never gets old.

Let's talk about ghosts. Thousands of workers died during the copper mining heydays, and the general consensus is that pretty much all of them have stuck around the area in some incorporeal form. Jerome has been considered the most haunted town in America, and while I'm not quite sure that's something you can qualify, there's no denying that there's something unsettling about the town. At one point, the Chamber of Commerce would report the latest round of sightings in their newsletter, getting enough to take up the back page.

If you are a fan of the paranormal, try to book a room at the Grand Hotel at the top of town. At one time known as the United Verde Hospital, it was where upwards of 9,000 died during the town's mining heyday until its closure in 1950. And just like any good horror movie, this old hospital was renovated nearly half a century later into the Grand Hotel, now considered by those in the know to be the single-most haunted building in the entire state.

I've heard more personal stories come from "encounters" at this hotel than from anywhere else in town, and that's saying something. Want to have your faucet turn on in the middle of the night? Have your comforter yanked off and thrown on the floor? Dodge floating orbs and listen to the sound of squeaking gurneys rolled down hallways? Then book a room here. Ask for #32 if you're a total masochist.

I do not believe in ghosts. I'm firmly in the "rational explanation for what's perceived as paranormal" camp. That being said, I'll be honest with you - I've had three experiences in my life, all of them in Jerome, that I cannot begin to explain. For example, one night I was visiting the town late at night, and I walked up to a tiny park across from the saloon. I was completely alone, and I sat down on a swing to rock a bit and look at the stars.

At the time, there wasn't the slightest bit of a breeze, but directly to my left I heard a small laugh and saw the swing start to move forward and backward, faster and higher with each swing, until it was topping out at four or five feet in the air. I watched this whole thing because I was absolutely frozen solid in a moment where the rules of the universe no longer seemed to apply, and it took a good ten seconds before I could take control of my limbs and get the hell out of there. The other stories are longer and more disconcerting.

There are some fantastic shops and galleries through town, as well as some of my favorite restaurants outside of Sedona. I recommend The Haunted Hamburger, Grapes and Vaqueros. Check out The Mine Cafe for breakfast if you're up early to beat the crowd. Grab a drink at Paul & Jerry's Saloon, the oldest family-owned saloon in Arizona, or grab a drink and catch some fun live and local music at the legendary Spirit Room. And my favorite restaurant, the more upscale Asylum, is on the ground floor of the aforementioned mega-haunted Grand Hotel. Get reservations here and jockey for a seat near a window to combine ridiculous views and fantastic food. If the butternut squash soup is available, get four bowls of it (or at least one).

If you make it to Jerome, I highly recommend the short drive out to Gold King Mine. Accessible via Perkinsville Rd. to the right of the fire department on Main St., this tourist attraction is overloaded with remnants of the mining days. It's a barely organized mess of hundreds of fascinating things, including equipment, vehicles and buildings of the time.

The haphazardness of it lends to its beautiful weirdness and fascination and is well worth the modest price of admission. If you're going to stay at the Grand Hotel, or one of the nice B&B's in town, go visit the Gold King Mine's shed of dangling chainsaws to help you sleep better that night. I love this place.

In closing, just go to Jerome. It's awesome fun. To get there, take 89A west from Sedona to Cottonwood, about a fifteen minute drive. When you get to Cottonwood St., you have two options. If you turn left, you'll stay on 89A, which will lead you straight to Jerome, another 4 mile drive. When you reach the final roundabout, take it around past the gas station to begin your climb up the hill.

Your second option, the more scenic of the two, is to remain on Main St., which is what 89A is known when you reach Cottonwood. This drive will take you through Old Town, which is a newly-renovated and worthwhile spot to take in if you're in the area. If you can stop, you should, but simply driving through and taking in some more of the area is worth it. This road will take you along the Verde River, past the Tuzigoot ruins off into the distance to your right, and into the tiny village of Clarkdale.

This is another neat little town to drive through, and while I personally don't stop and wander the town, I do like checking it out from time to time. You'll stay on the main road until you reach the park, where you'll take a left on 11th St and turn 45 degrees onto Clarkdale Parkway. From here it's less than a quarter mile to the roundabout where you'll meet back up with 89A and head to Jerome.

Arcosanti

If you'd like to explore an urban living experiment ripped right out of a science fiction movie, you need to take a tour of Arcosanti. The brainchild of renowned Italian Architect Paolo Soleri, who studied with Frank Lloyd Wright, this continually-growing "urban laboratory" hosts anywhere from 50 to 150 inhabitants at any given time who are continuing its gradual expansion.

The tours are very interesting if you have any sort of interest in progressive thinking and/or architecture, and the whole experience is wonderfully surreal. Check the calendar for events, as they hold concerts in their gloriously trippy amphitheater.

If you're into photography, there's never enough time to document all the beautiful and unique structures while in the complex, but you'll have time to capture as a whole. There's a trail from the visitors' center to the south, and a short walk will give you an outstanding vista of the project.

If you're REALLY into this kind of stuff, Arcosanti offers overnight lodging from dorm-style to their very well-accommodated Sky Suite. Staying as an overnight guest gives you fairly unrestricted access to the complex, giving you ample time to explore this honestly fascinating and wildly unique location in the high desert.

The Ruins

Montezuma's Castle

This is my favorite cliff dwelling in the area and the one I think is most impressive. Estimated to be between 600 and 1000 years old, this 4,000 sq. ft., five story structure was built by the Sinagua approximately 90 feet up the cliff. To get there, take Highway 179 south of VOC to I-17, then head south about ten miles to the Middle Verde Rd. exit. Follow the signs to the casino and you can't miss it. Stay on this road and just past the casino you'll see Montezuma Castle Rd. on your left, and it's less than a mile to the Castle visitors' center.

Montezuma's Well

I've been consistently underwhelmed by this location, but it definitely holds interest for those who appreciate the history of the area and the Sinagua tribe. They built a small cliff dwelling around the edge of a 400 ft. wide sinkhole that is constantly filled by an underground spring. A combination of its location and appeal to the average visitor makes me suggest this as an option more for those especially interested in the ancient tribes of the area. There are two ways to reach the well - first is by taking Highway 179 south of VOC to I-17, crossing underneath the highway and heading down this road a quarter mile to Montezuma Well Rd. You'll find the entrance to the well about four miles down a dirt road that's easily accessible by passenger vehicle.

The second way to get there is to take I-17 south of Highway 179 to the McGuireville/Montezuma Well exit about five miles south. Right after exiting you'll turn right on Cornville Rd then follow this around as it turns into Beaver Creek Rd. This road will take you through the small town of Rimrock, and the paved section will end at the well. This is a good option if you don't feel like taking the dirt road (I have friends who drive sports cars who won't take them off pavement, so I understand) but it's a fair amount of extra time to take this way. If you're coming from Montezuma's Well and want to tack this on, though, this is the way to go.

Palatki and Honanki

I'm grouping these sites together, as they are fairly similar and only a mile from one another. Both of these sites consist of substantial remnants of cliff dwellings nestled within outstanding red rock scenery. They're just distinct enough to warrant visiting both if you're into history, but you could get by with visiting only one if you're just after the experience. In addition to the cliff dwellings, you can find some pretty fascinating pictographs left behind by the Sinagua. Accessibility to the actual dwellings can vary - I've been able to take a tour of the actual rooms before, and then later visits found that concerns over structural weakening kept visitors a hundred feet from them. So don't go to either anticipating full access, although it's possible they'll offer it. Of the two, Palatki is closer to the main drive.

Both are accessible out past Dry Creek Rd., which turns into a Forest Service Rd. You'll have to take a dirt road that any passenger vehicle can take and are open to the public. I'm not going to attempt to give you directions here, as the roads out here can get fairly confusing. This is a situation where it's ideal to have someone reading a physical map, or one on their phone. There are signs along the way that'll help guide you in to either. While you can access these from Forest Rd. 525, intersecting 89A about a mile and a half outside West Sedona, it's worth taking the Dry Creek Rd./Boynton Pass Rd. way out for the considerably more interesting scenery.

Tuzigoot

This is one of the more impressive remnants of the Sinagua culture and is worth the drive out, especially combined with a trip to Jerome, which is right up the road from here. This pueblo, at one time 3 stories tall and consisting of 110 rooms, is remarkably intact. You can walk right up to the thousand-year old walls and get a full appreciation of the construction savvy these people possessed. The Visitors' Center has a very impressive collection of artifacts recovered from the site as well.

To get to Tuzigoot from Sedona, take 89A west to Cottonwood, staying on this road as it turns to Main St. in town. Drive through Old Town and head toward Clarkdale about one mile until you see Tuzigoot Rd. On your right. You'll get a view of the Verde River here and some great views of Clarkdale, Jerome and Mingus Mountain as well.

Wupatki - Special Mention

If you are particularly interested in what the Sinagua culture has left behind for us to explore, I have to mention that my favorite spot by far, Wupatki, is about 90 minutes north of Sedona. This 100-room pueblo is the most interesting and beatiful of all of them to me, and it's particularly striking where it lies on the wide, sage-dotted stretches north of Flagstaff. It also has an excellent visitors' center. It's a commitment to get up there, but if you are fascinated by these structures, consider making the drive up.

The quickest way to get there is to take 89A up through the canyon, or I-17, to I-40 and head to the east until you reach Country Club Dr. in Flagstaff. Take a right on 89 less than ten miles to the Sunset Crater/Wupatki entrance. From there, it's another 15 miles or so to Wupatki.

Cliff Castle Casino

I come from a family with many members who feel compelled to seek out nickel slots if they're within a reasonable driving distance. Therefore, I must mention that Cliff Castle Casino is a nice option for rolling the literal dice, not too far from Sedona. You'll take Highway 179 south of VOC to I-17, and take that highway south about ten miles to Middle Verde Rd. where you'll find the casino right off the highway to your south. As per the rules of casinos, you'll be reminded of its existence via outdoor advertising enough to where there's a 0% chance of missing it.

Flagstaff and the Grand Canyon

Flagstaff

To many of us, Flagstaff (just called "Flag" around here) is primarily our "big city". We have Phoenix for when we need access to absolutely everything we could ever want, and we have Cottonwood for the essentials, but Flagstaff has what I'd consider the minimum level of everything I'll need. There are some fantastic restaurants in Flag, and the downtown area is particularly entertaining, but because I'm accustomed to small town life, a trip up the canyon is usually to get what I need and get out.

What does pull me up the canyon for fun times are opportunities to play in the mountains. Skiing is an obvious one, and many flock to the Snow Bowl when the snow is good (and it often gets absolutely wonderful up there), but for me, I prefer to head up when the weather is nice to check out one of two areas.

First, I absolutely adore the views and trails around the Snow Bowl area. I'll head up to the Humphreys trail head for the absolutely killer views and hiking among the aspens. It's a significant change in terrain from what I'm accustomed to, and the temperature swing can be a big deal - if you visit Sedona during one of the warmer months, a trip up to Humphreys Peak can bring temps 20-30 degrees cooler, ideal for outdoor activities. I particularly like the Arizona Trail leading from Humphreys Peak Trail parking area, as well as the namesake trail.

To get to the Snow Bowl area and Humphreys trail head, take 89A up the canyon and get on I-17 at the roundabout, or just take I-17 via Highway 179 south of VOC. 17 turns into Milton Rd. when you reach Flag. Stay on Milton for a little over a mile, and when the road takes a sharp turn to the left, take a left on Humphreys St. right by the downtown area.

Take this road a few blocks up to Columbus Avenue and take a left, where it becomes N. Fort Valley Rd, which you'll take for about 5-6 miles to Snow Bowl Rd. This meandering drive up the mountain will end up at the Snow Bowl, and you'll want to take the first parking area on your left when you get up there. The views from up here are nuts.

My other favorite place to check out is Lockett Meadow. This meadow, campground and starting point for the Inner Basin Trail is far up into the San Francisco Peaks, and is a stunning place to explore. In the spring, the wildflowers can be sublime, and in the fall the yellow aspens are a work of art. I'm a huge fan of the Inner Basin Trail, so if you'd like to do some high elevation hiking, it's worth reading up on.

I've seen many passenger cars reach the meadow, but I'll warn you that the drive can seem a little perilous. You'll want to get to I-40 via 89A or I-17 and head east a few miles to Country Club Dr., where you'll take a right on Highway 89. From there, it's a good 15-20 minute drive. When you see the sign for Sunset Crater, you'll want to be in the left lane, as you'll take the crossover to the left opposite this entrance. The road becomes gravel right after you cross over the highway.

Take your first right at the T and your second right after that, which has signage for the meadow. At this point, the road becomes the kind you don't take your eyes off of. It's a lot of elevation changes and twists/turns, just wide enough for two cars to pass, and rough gravel. Take your sweet time making the climb up and you'll be amply rewarded at the end.

The Grand Canyon

I will never forget my first time seeing the Grand Canyon. I distinctly remember walking from the parking area with no canyon in sight, just trees, disappointed to be so close and yet have no payoff. And then I abruptly arrived at the rim, totally, thoroughly unprepared for the "words incapable of doing justice" sensory overload that rocked me. All I could do was stand there and laugh, thinking "No way..." repeatedly as I tried to make sense of what I was seeing.

Sedona is heartbreakingly beautiful but the Grand Canyon exists on an entirely different level of reality. If you're in the area and have never been, figure out how you can get up there. And if you've been before, figure out a way to go again. I just can't begin to imagine an experience on our planet more profound than gazing across the depths of that miracle.

It seems that well over 90% of visitors to the Grand Canyon head to the South Rim via Tusayan to get their fix. I'll be the first to say there's nothing wrong with this, mainly because it's the Grand Canyon and there's no wrong way to see it. However, over the past 19 years, I grew increasingly frustrated with experiencing it from this vantage point.

Being the primary stop for almost all visitors meant an often overwhelming number of visitors, many of which were brought in by bus, and each observation area was overrun and occasionally impassable. It was hard to enjoy a view partially obstructed by a wall of cameras and cell phones being held as high as arms would go, with hundreds of conversations happening simultaneously. It felt more like Disneyland than a national park. And then I learned about Desert View Drive and the canyon became incredibly special to me again.

If you look at a map of the Grand Canyon, you'll see that the area almost all visitors wind up at, with the Village and visitors' center, provides you with incredible views across the canyon. But with something so incredibly long, you feel like you're missing out on looking down it. Now follow Highway 64, or Desert View Dr. as it turns to the east right before the main visitors' area. You'll see that it follows the canyon as it turns north, with observation points along the way to help you appreciate this beautiful space in a whole new way.

Another compelling reason to see the canyon from along this road is the aforementioned fight for an unobstructed spot to take in the views. If you're anything like me, the overwhelming crowds can detract from that connection with nature, but the good (fantastic) news is they don't venture very far from the main visitors' area. I've been there many times when it's too crowded to enjoy from Yavapai Point, a stone's throw from the main visitors' center, but by driving a few miles down Desert View Rd. I can find an observation area where I'm literally the only person there.

So here's my recommendation: skip the main area and drive east. Or, if you are just hellbent on getting the full experience, budget time for both, spending considerably less time around the main area than you might otherwise. Shortly after you start down Desert View Rd. you'll find Yaki Point.

About ten miles down you'll hit the turnoff for Grandview Point, then another ten or so and you'll reach my personal favorites, Lipan Point and Desert View Watchtower. When you're this far down the road, it's highly likely you'll only have a handful of visitors to contend with at most, and the unique vantage point these spots offer provide some of the best views available.

The quick and dirty plan is always to drive to the main canyon area via Tusayan, take in the views and come back the same way. It's probably the most efficient way to scratch a visit off the bucket list. But my recommendation is to budget more time and make a loop of it by following this plan:

Leave Flagstaff to the northeast on 89 and head about 60 miles north to where it meets Desert View Drive. There's ample signage in the area to make sure you don't miss it. You'll drive another 30 miles to reach the canyon itself. Along this drive you'll pay the entrance fee, which is currently $30 per vehicle. Your first pullout, at the watchtower, will be on your right - start here and then stop at each one along the way to the west. You'll run into the main visitors' area at the end. Stay on Highway 64 south through the main entrance and into the town of Tusayan, then south about 20 miles to the turnoff for Highway 180 near Bedrock City and the Grand Canyon Inn.

From here it's roughly an hour back to Flagstaff, with great views of the San Francisco Peaks waiting for you at the end. I like doing the loop in this direction, as there's more desert to take in on 89 north, and there's not much scenery along 180. I'm usually coming back around or after sunset so I don't feel like I'm missing anything. If you take this route, follow the Snow Bowl directions in the Flagstaff section in reverse to get back to I-17 and 89A down the canyon.

This drive will put you on the road considerably longer than a straight "drive up, look and drive back" trip, and if that's all you have the time for, then do it. That's how I did my first trip up and don't regret a thing. But if you really want to experience more of what the canyon has to offer, I strongly recommend figuring out some way to enjoy the views along Desert View, as it's how the canyon is supposed to be admired as far as I'm concerned.

Regarding the North Rim: Since almost all tourism at the Grand Canyon takes place at the South Rim, I'm focusing on that in the guide. The South Rim offers more vantage points and is significantly closer to Sedona. Also, the North Rim is only open from May to October. If you are after the most solitude, the North Rim will certainly give it to you, as it only gets 10% of all visitors to the canyon, but I love the views and variety of the South Rim lookouts so much that I don't think the North Rim is a crucial part of the experience.

Dangerous Encounters

Wildlife Encounters

Sedona, lying in the middle of the nearly 2-million-acre Coconino National Forest, sees abundant wildlife year round. You'll likely see rabbits and the much larger jackrabbits, coyotes and javelina while in town, occasionally running into pronghorn antelope and other larger animals outside the town's boundaries. There is also an abundance of snakes, insects and lizards you'll encounter along trails. While the vast majority of wildlife encounters are completely harmless, there is the potential on any given day for dangerous situations to arise, so here are the types of wildlife you'll want to be aware of and keep an eye out for.

Javelina

Javelina, another term for peccary, are very common in this part of the state. While the babies are positively adorable and about the size of a loaf of bread, adults commonly grow to 4 ft. in length and weigh just shy of 100 lb. Like any wildlife, your typical encounter will send them scurrying frantically, but there have been a number of encounters with tourists over the years that have ended poorly. Over the years there have been reports of visitors finding the javelina to be cute or fascinating and making an effort to pet or interact with them.

It goes without saying that it's never a good idea to approach any wildlife - lately there have been some cases of rabies found in the rodent family up in the canyon, so even the smallest and cutest animals around should be avoided. But the javelina in particular should be avoided for one simple reason - their tusks. Some of those misguided tourists who have tried to get close to the javelina have been gored by their tusks and needed to be rushed to the ER.

Since I arrived in the area nearly 20 years ago, I have had literally hundreds of encounters with javelina, and by being smart about each one, I've never come close to experiencing a threatening situation. I've stumbled across packs of a dozen or more while hiking, and by keeping my distance and making loud noises I've consistently scared them into the trees.

The biggest danger I feel they present is when driving at night. I almost always see them venture out of the forest after sunset, wandering into town to forage for food. They're oblivious to traffic, and I've come close to hitting them dozens of times. Since the town hardly has any street lights, they appear quickly in your headlights when driving the speed limit, so when driving anywhere outside the main areas of West Sedona or the Village of Oak Creek, be extra vigilant to keep your eyes on the road constantly. Hitting an adult javelina at 40+ MPH can do some serious damage to a car and completely take out a motorcyclist.

Snakes

I've seen hundreds of snakes while hiking and driving the back roads around the area, and depending on what time of year you're here, there's a good chance you could find some as well. Many are not venomous - we have gopher snakes and ground snakes, and the king snake is welcomed due to its propensity for eating rattlesnakes. But unless you're very familiar with the different types of snakes in the area, it's a good rule of thumb to treat them all as if they're venomous. And by that, I don't suggest injuring them in any way, as they all have their place in the ecosystem. Rather, if you do encounter one, give it a wide berth.

The most common venomous snakes in the area are rattlers, but you can't count on them warning you of their presence. Be mindful of where you step, especially when crossing on or over logs or rocks that offer them some protection. Also be careful where you put your hands when rock scrambling.

Insects

Dangerous things with many legs lurk all over the area. Scorpions, spiders, centipedes and millipedes can be found all throughout town as well as the wilderness, so be mindful of their presence. I've encountered all of these inside my home, including scorpions inside shoes and boots. All it takes is one encounter like this to make you shake footwear upside down thoroughly before putting them on your feet. If you are coming to camp and you leave your boots outside, it's an especially good idea to give them a good shake before slipping them on. We have Arizona bark scorpions in the area, a particularly nasty type, so it's never a bad idea to check everywhere you can before settling in, indoors or out.

Tarantulas were nightmare fodder for me until I moved out here and learned how little I needed to worry about them. I see a handful every month, and you could encounter one in town or in the wilderness. The varieties we have around here are fairly harmless, with venom weaker than a bee sting. As far as things to be wary of, these are actually low on the list. Regardless, it's still a good idea to refrain from trying to pick them up or pet them, which many tourists have attempted over the years.

What has taken their place as a very scary encounter is the tarantula hawk, a type of wasp occasionally seen in the area. These are about two inches long, with blue-black bodies and rust-colored wings. If you do happen to see what you think could be one, make every effort to put distance between it and you. The tarantula wasp has what is considered to be the most painful sting of any insect alive today.

The pain is described as so severe that you're literally incapable of rational thought for a good two to five minutes, and all you can do is just lie down and scream until the pain passes. While the sting isn't particularly dangerous to humans and rarely requires medical attention, the descriptions and videos documenting the incredible pain from one of these wasps is more than enough to make me keep my eyes peeled for one while outside.

Coyotes

Many a beautiful evening here has been accentuated by the forlorn melodies of the many coyotes in the area. It's a quintessential southwest experience to hear their songs and the responses of others in the distance. Coyotes themselves are essentially harmless little things, scared to death of people, and you'll likely only see one as a darting blur in your headlights.

Where they do pose a danger is with your pets. These pack animals are smart, and they have ways to lure canine companions into unfortunate situations. I've heard time and again about a hiker's dog seeing a lone coyote on a trail and chasing after it enthusiastically, only to be led into an ambush by the coyote's pack. These dogs never stand a chance in these situations. It almost feels criminal to abide by the leash laws when bringing your dog hiking, as you want them to run and play and enjoy the experience as much as you do. But be very aware that leashes can save your dog's life, especially if it's a smaller breed, when hiking where hungry coyotes are lurking.

Elk

These massive, beautiful creatures are fairly common in the higher elevations. I've seen them almost exclusively between the top of Oak Creek Canyon and Flagstaff and along the dirt roads in the wilderness east of I-17 and south of I-40. While essentially harmless, the greatest threat they possess is when driving highway speeds.

Many people have seen what can happen when a vehicle collides with something as small as a whitetail deer, so imagine the damage or risk of injury if the animal that appears in the middle of the road is the size of a small horse. Twenty or thirty times I've been driving 50 while heading to Flagstaff in the dark and have rounded a bend to see five or six adult elk standing on the highway. I've seen some that don't immediately bolt, and it can take some quick reflexes to ensure your safety.

Bears and Mountain Lions

Just be aware that both have been spotted in the area, exclusively in high elevations in the rocks north of town from my understanding. While sightings of each have been so infrequent as to fall into legend, it's smart to be aware that there's a slim chance you'll encounter one or the other. If you're hardcore about trail safety, at a minimum you can educate yourself on how to react to these encounters, or you can get hardcore and carry bear spray or some other deterrent with you.

Weather

Much of this is touched upon in the "Best Time to Visit" section, so I won't repeat it verbatim here, but will focus on immediate concerns in the area. A big one for those unaccustomed to summer heat is dehydration. Where I'm from, the high humidity can lead to considerable sweat stains, a clear indicator of how much vital water your body is using to cool itself.

Out here, the humidity can get so low that the sweat can evaporate before it soaks into clothing, so I wound up dry during long hikes. Just because you don't see the usual effects of physical exertion doesn't mean you aren't losing fluids. Hydration is essential around here, so make sure you are carrying, and consuming, a significant amount of water while enjoying the out of doors.

During monsoon season, and when snow melt up the canyon starts to fill Oak Creek, flooding can occur throughout town and the surrounding area. It's common knowledge not to drive into flood waters, but I feel the need to reiterate that point here. There's always another way to get where you're going, so if you see rushing water over a roadway, don't begin to think it's worth risking it and trying to cross. If you find yourself in this situation, find someone to give you directions on the scenic route back.

One point I will revisit is the snow. I can't stress how bad it can get on the highways, so if you're out here during the winter months, I strongly advise you not to consider driving up the canyon or I-17 unless the Arizona Department of Public Safety explicitly states the roads are passable.

Easily the most terrifying times in my life, absent any hyperbole whatsoever, were attempting to return to Sedona when snow was falling around and south of Flagstaff. It's hard to overstate how quickly the snow can accumulate and how treacherous driving can become. Please play it as safe as possible and avoid driving anywhere snow is quickly accumulating.

AZ511.gov offers near-real-time webcams of highways, so if you have access to the internet you can use this resource to get an excellent understanding of almost any area you're heading.

Uncertain Footing While Hiking

As someone accustomed to hiking across the sure footing of granite, I was not prepared for how treacherous exploring the red rocks can be around here. While the trails are almost always perfectly fine to travel on, I've been in higher elevation areas with much loose rock on sloping areas. No matter how well my boots could grip, these surfaces caused me to lose my footing unless I went very slow. This isn't a great area to hike with hands in pockets as there are some areas that can send you tumbling much easier than you think. There are far too many inclines around here to put yourself in a situation where you could slide down them, so be extra careful where and how you step.

The Tourist Invasion

Those of us who have lived here for some time generally have a love/hate relationship with the tourism industry. Most of the town, and the greater Verde Valley area, depend on the roughly 4 million visitors we see each year to show up with your checkbooks and credit cards. We've seen spending increase to around $600 million a year, taxes on which are most of what keeps the city functional. So most understand how utterly vital your visits are. Without you, many wouldn't have the opportunity to live in such a spectacularly amazing place.

But all those visitors have a distinct downside that spoil some, or much, of the joy of living among the red rocks. Each spring and fall we have millions of people showing up in a town of ten thousand. Traffic during peak times has the potential to become positively unreal - for some living in the Village of Oak Creek, it can take 45 minutes to drive the four or five miles to their jobs in Sedona, with Highway 179 devolving into essentially a parking lot. From the intersection of 179 and 89A, just south of Uptown, we can see the same slowdowns, backing roads up for miles. Many ignore speed limits, drive drunk, block driveways - just make themselves an unabashed nuisance for too many.

Many complain about where the money goes, as well. While $600 million is a massive number, much of that is spent on lodging at hotel chains that funnel that money out of the state or country. Sedona winds up seeing only the initial land purchase, bed taxes and wages staying around town, a tiny fraction of what is spent. With the increase in tourism comes an increased interest in taking advantage of it, and what little land is available is constantly chased for development. Our views are slowly eaten away by bigger hotels. Our favorite local spots are razed to make condos and timeshares.

You can rest assured that any given person who relocated to Sedona did so to experience the land. We want to do the same things you do - hike a trail, go to Slide Rock, hit a bar. And we want to do it when the tourists do. From March to May and From September to November, the weather is so stunning that we want to get out among the red rocks, only to find that every single day, every single parking spot at every single trailhead is occupied by those from out of town. The parking spots at our favorite restaurants are completely filled from open to close. It's extremely disheartening to realize that your ability to enjoy the world-famous aspects of your hometown is taken away by the very reasons it thrives.

And as of late tourism has had an especially vicious impact on the town. Lately Arizona changed a law concerning renting properties short-term, allowing for many property owners and managers to move away from monthly rentals to cater to the AirBnB crowd. Their potential income by doing so increases significantly, so what is undeniably a smart business decision has utterly devastated rental opportunities for locals.

Many hundreds of individuals and families found their landlords converting to short-term and no longer renewing leases or breaking them entirely. What little that remained has been too expensive for many who have been here for years, forcing them to move to other locations in the Verde Valley. Stores that cater to locals, like grocery stores and cleaners, saw a drop in sales.

With so many children pulled out of town, some smaller schools are being pushed to financial instability. And when emergencies happen, and we need more than those on shift to take them on, we see our police, fire, and EMTs having to travel 30 minutes to join in. Our wonderful little town is becoming less self-sufficient, less contained, less of a home and more of an amusement park, and it's breaking hearts all over.

How can you be a better tourist?

Pack Out Your Trash - We come along behind the seasonal juggernaut of tourism to discover the trails we are deeply in love with are spoiled by a surprising amount of litter. Leaving trash along a trail side is, and should be considered unconscionable! If you're able to bring it with you from your car, you're able to bring it back. And if you want to earn a little extra karma along the way, help us keep the trails pristine by snagging any trash you see along the way.

Be Conscientious - The speed limit is 35 through much of the town. Parking spaces are diamond-rare of many days. Turn signals were invented for a reason. While you're here, please be mindful of what's going on around you. Drive courteously, park carefully to only take up one space and park tightly at trailheads. Oh, and under NO CIRCUMSTANCES should you ever think of carving your initials, or anything for that matter, in the red rocks. It gets reported, people will make sure to get car tags and whatnot, and the law will go after many people each year for doing this. Don't risk it. The only thing you're allowed to leave behind in Sedona is your money.

And please keep in mind that since tourism causes such a significant amount of problems here, our police force doesn't mess around. DUIs and moving violations are handed out daily. We have a very alert police force, so don't give them a reason to pay attention to you.

A note about driving - many people are used to streetlights covering every square inch of their city and are surprised to see how truly dark it can get here. During a new moon, I can walk outside at certain points and not see a car parked on the curb. We have all sorts of wildlife around here, such as deer, coyote and wild peccaries known as javelina. You need to be extra alert while driving, save all distractions for when the car is in park, and for the love of God, don't try to navigate the town's twists and turns in the dark if you've been drinking. Too many tourists die and/or kill unsuspecting locals because of the extra challenges they aren't sober enough to face. We have taxis, Uber, a nice local within earshot - there's always a safe way to get back to where you're staying. Do not ever EVER drink and drive for all our sakes.

Be Friendly - For some reason, people seem to develop a sense of entitlement the moment they arrive in town. Being on vacation seems to instill in some an idea that they can be short, rude and selfish while on vacation. Do not be one of these people under any circumstances. You'll be appreciated so much by just letting the excitement and peace that comes from being in town come through every interaction here.

Remember, there are likely many times the population of town as tourists at any given moment, and everyone is rushed. Tables at restaurants can require a wait. Staff will likely be juggling a lot. You can't expect everything to work out your way in a town this busy. Many issues will just fall under an "it is what it is" scenario, with nothing anyone can do, so just focus on what you can put your positive energy into and shrug off the frustrations that occasionally occur here.

Another way friendliness can pay off - talk to a local! Many of us remember what it was like when we came to visit before we moved, and we can appreciate someone else in that moment. If you don't know where to go, what to check out, when is the best time for any given activity, feel comfortable asking. It's nice to step outside the vendor/customer relationship and have a real conversation with someone who truly wants to enjoy their experience here. I love being able to help someone create moments they'll remember for a long time, and many others feel the same way. Don't be shy about making a quick friend or two while you're here.

Made in the USA
Coppell, TX
30 October 2022

85473514R00042